Let There Be Thought

Eira Quinn

Content Warning

This collection includes references to:

- Religious trauma, indoctrination, and spiritual abuse

- Homophobia, transphobia, and queerphobia (including references to violence and erasure)

- Misogyny, purity culture, and gender-based oppression

- Sexual violence and coercion

- Domestic abuse and theological justifications for it

- Suicidal ideation and the deaths of marginalized individuals

- Child indoctrination and fear-based teachings around hell and damnation

- Systemic injustice involving race, class, gender, and identity

- Existential fear and the emotional fallout of deconstruction

If you need support, resources are included in the back of the book. You are not alone.

Reader's Note

A portion of these pieces come from my own reckoning with the idea of God. What it demanded, what it distorted, what it cost. Others are shaped by the anger and grief of people I've witnessed refusing to disappear.

Some of these words will feel sharp. Some may feel like a wound reopening. That is not because truth is cruel, but because cruelty was once called truth.

This book was written with anger, and with love. It is not meant to be an attack of belief itself, but to challenge the ways belief has been weaponized in order to silence, shame, and control.

If you find yourself uncomfortable here, I invite you to pause, to breathe, and to ask;
is this discomfort harmful? Or is it the sound of a system breaking open?

You are welcome to wrestle with what you find. You are welcome to put the book down when you need to. I offer these pages not as a map, but as a mirror. May you find yourself, and your freedom, in the reflection.

The old gods demanded your fear. Here, we ask only for your truth.

— Eira Quinn

***

A reader's guide with annotations, biblical references, and a glossary of key terms is available at eiraquinn.com/annotations

Contents

LET THERE BE THOUGHT

Poems

by Eira Quinn

For my younger self.

For the questioners.

[I]

Subjugation

Born into chains you never chose.

If You're There

Dear God,
I don't believe in you,
but I grew up knowing your name.

You say *knock and the door will be opened.*
But it's not a door, it's a courtroom.
One where the judge already knows my name,
and the sentence was written before I ever spoke.

Your people—
They wear your name like a crown
and wield it like a sword.
They shout about life
but leave no room for the living.

I've seen what they do in your name.
How they twist scripture like barbed wire
and string it across voting booths.

I've seen the prayers that come with policies.
The grace that stops
at borders and bathrooms.
The mercy that expires
when someone says they're gay.

I don't believe in you,

but sometimes I want to.
Not the judge in the sky with a gavel and a grudge,
but someone better.

Because if you're real
I need you to be more than judgment and power.
More than the smoke machines and slurs.
More than a verse quoted
while they pass the bill that kills someone like me.

I hope you're angry.
I hope you're weeping.
I hope you're ready to flip tables again
and ask them why they turned your house
into a machine for shame.

Fire Insurance

We were warned early.
Told that heaven waited
if we obeyed,
and hell burned
if we slipped.

Some were just learning to speak,
mouthing bedtime prayers
like insurance policies,
whispering apologies
for thoughts they didn't yet understand.

But I've already seen
what their hell looks like.
And it doesn't look like fire.

It looks like a family crossing a desert,
blisters blooming on their feet,
no papers in their pockets.
Only hope.

It looks like a trans child
brave enough to live her truth,
while grown men
debate her right to breathe.

It looks like prayers
used as policies.
Votes used as violence.
Budgets written like death sentences.

They warned us about hell.
But hell is here.
Built by ballots.
Carved by laws.
Preached into existence.

We built it ourselves.
We stoke it every day.

And still,
they dare to call this holy.

Exit Wound

What better way
to make people stay
than to threaten them
with eternal pain?

They say it's justice.
That love can be proven
through fire.

But ask yourself:
What kind of god
creates children
with soft hearts
and open hands
only to burn them
for being human?

What kind of mercy
damns a soul
for asking questions?

What kind of justice
requires forever
to punish a moment?

If love must be feared,

is it love at all?

If salvation means silence,
who does it save?

If hell is the price
of being alive,
then your god
makes monsters
of us all.

The Women They Don't Preach About

You know the ones.
Always early, always serving.
The ones who brewed the coffee,
folded the bulletins,
sang in the choir
and swallowed their questions
with communion wine.

They don't preach about them.
Don't mention the Sunday school girls
taught to be modest
before they even knew
what they were sacrificing.

They don't mention the woman
who led Bible study for forty years
but never stood behind a pulpit
because Paul said *no*.

They don't mention the wives
who prayed through black eyes
and miscarriages,
and were told
God hates divorce
more than he hates your pain.

They don't mention
the teenage girls given purity rings
instead of consent,
whose worth was measured
in white dresses
and shame.

They called it *womanhood.*
They called it *calling.*
They called it *faith.*

But what they really meant
was *silence.*
Was *labor.*
Was *second place*
with a smile.

Those women carried the
whole damn church
on their backs
and were still told
to sit down
and listen.

Mary Couldn't Consent

We're told she was favored.
Chosen.
Blessed among women.

But she was just a child.
And *chosen* doesn't mean *safe*.
Blessed doesn't always mean *I wanted this*.

The story says an angel came—
Bright. Beautiful. Terrifying—
and said *you will bear a son*.

Not a question.
A command.

And she nodded.
Because what else do you do
when the divine speaks over you?

They made her obedience into a miracle.
Said it proved her purity.
Her worth.
Her womanhood.

But no one asked
how it felt

to have your future rewritten
by a voice that would not wait
for your answer.

They called it holy.
But I call it familiar.
I call it every woman
who's been told
you should be grateful.

They made her silence scripture.
Built entire theologies
on her closed mouth
and lowered eyes.

But what if Mary had screamed
I'm too young.
I'm afraid.
I don't want this.

Would they still have called it sacred?

Or would they have buried it
like so many other girls
whose pain didn't fit
the prophecy?

Sunday School

They told me about Noah,
but not the bodies.
Not the screaming
beneath rising water,
or the mothers
who begged God for mercy
as he watched from the clouds
and said nothing.

I heard about Job,
but they skipped the bet.
The part where God let the Devil
ruin a man's life
just to prove a point.
Killed his children.
Stripped his skin.
And called it *righteous testing*.

They told me about Abraham's faith,
but not Isaac's trauma.
Not what it does to a boy
to see his father raise a knife
with heaven's approval.
Not the silence that follows
when you survive a god
who wanted you dead.

No one mentioned the concubines,
the raped,
the forgotten wives,
the daughters sold
for the price of land
or peace
or power.

They didn't talk about
stoning disobedient sons,
or killing gay lovers,
or what to do
if a woman is not a virgin
on her wedding night.

They said Jesus died for us,
but not that God
could've chosen forgiveness
without blood.
That maybe the crucifixion
wasn't salvation,
but spectacle.

They said *trust the Word,*
but they handed me
a censored book
and a list of acceptable questions.
And when I asked

about the rest,
they said *have faith.*

But faith without truth
is just fear
in nicer clothing.

And now that I've read
what they skipped—
now that I've seen
what they hid—
I can't go back
to coloring pages
and quiet amens.

The god they taught me
was edited.
Redacted.
Rebranded.

But the truth?
The truth was always there.
In the margins.
In the footnotes.
In the blood.

Built in His Image, Then Blamed for It

Creation, they claim, was intentional.
Every flawed chromosome.
Every system that breaks
under the weight of being born.
Predators in nature.
Tumors in toddlers.

He made it,
then called it *good*.

He gave us choice,
but tied consequences to eternity.
He gave us free will
with a trapdoor.

Love me, or burn.
Obey me, or fall.

Still, they call him *just*.
Still, they call him *Father*.
Even when fatherhood looks like punishment
disguised as protection.

They say he loves us.
But what kind of love
requires a surveillance system?

What kind of mercy
comes with a clause?

He cursed the first woman
for wanting to know.
Turned curiosity into treason.
Branded freedom
as rebellion.

And when we refuse to kneel,
they call us hell-bound.

Because we kissed the wrong lips.
Prayed to the wrong name.
Were born
on the wrong patch of earth.

And in their eyes,
that's enough.
Because hell isn't just for the cruel.
It's for the unconvinced.
And belief,
they say,
can bleach any bloodstained hands.

But if that's what God is,
a tyrant in robes,
a king who locks the gates

and blames the damned—
then I'll stand outside.

I'll leave the porch light on
for the ones he cast out.
I'll believe in love
that does not require
fear
to function.

THE BIBLE NOOSE

They called it armor.
Said it would keep her safe.

But it felt like a noose
tightening around her throat.

They named it the Bible Belt.
But it didn't hold up righteousness.
It held down girls
who talked too loud.
Boys who walked too gently.

It cinched tighter
with every verse quoted like a weapon.
Every rule carved into Sunday smiles.
Every whispered *bless her heart*
that meant *she doesn't belong.*

They wrapped it around the South
like it was heritage.
Like shame was a sacrament.

They say it keeps the country grounded.
But I've seen what it buries:
Science.
Sex ed.

Queer kids.
Women.
Truth.

And when it snaps—
because it always snaps—
they don't loosen it.
They blame the one
who couldn't breathe.

The Bible Belt is a noose
masquerading as morality.

It won't save you.
It will smile
while it tightens.
Say *this is love*
while you gasp.

[II]

Conflagration

Set fire to the lies they taught you.

Thread by Thread

The lesson was clear:
don't ask so many questions.

As though curiosity
is corruption.
As though asking questions
means I've failed a test
I never agreed to take.

Funny how the faith they preach
is so fragile
it can't survive a library.

They said *God is truth,*
but only if I stop reading
the fine print in the stories,
the contradictions in the red ink.

Only if I let fear
win the argument.

But I kept reading.
Kept thinking.
Kept following the thread
until it unraveled the whole damn thing.

GOD OF THE GAPS

We were all born
with curiosity in our veins,
and wonder in our bones.

Where awe failed,
we built gods.

The foragers had spirits.
The Greeks had Zeus.
The Norse had Odin.
The Egyptians had Ra.
The Mesopotamians had Marduk.
The Celts had Danu.
The Japanese had Amaterasu.
The Hebrews had Yahweh.

The gaps had gods;
the gods had gaps.

And when awe wasn't enough,
the clever ones built empires
profiting in gold
and in flesh.

But we became smarter.
Our tools, sharper.

Our maps, fuller.
Seasons explained.
Diseases named.
Earthquakes understood.

The realm of gods shrank
with every question answered,
every mystery translated
into human language.

The empire trembles now.
Built on the unknown,
threatened by discovery.

And So They Made Him a God

In the beginning,
there was a woman.
She bore life with her own hands
and fed the world from her body.
She built shelter from nothing
and filled it with heartbeat.

She was the origin story.
The fire. The flood. *The first word.*
And they hated her for it.

Because how do you conquer
what refuses to be claimed?

So they called her *dangerous.*
Carved her voice into silence.
Burned her wisdom with her body
and named the ashes sacred.

They took birth
and called it a curse.
Took her image from the heavens
and replaced it with a man on a throne.

Because it was easier to kneel
before something that looked like them.

So they rewrote the beginning.
Said *he* made the world.
Said *he* breathed life into dust.
Said woman came second—
from a rib, no less.

And just like that,
the one who created life
was made into a footnote.

But some of us remember
the stories written in stretch marks.
The hymns sung in lullabies.
The truth buried in our bloodlines.

We remember
that God was a woman
before they rewrote the script.

And no matter how loud they preach,
how hard they pray to the sky,
the earth still knows
who made her.

A Soul Lobotomized

I'm told in heaven
sorrow is impossible.
No grief.
No mourning.
No pain.

And when I asked
What about the ones I love?
The ones who didn't believe?
The ones you say are burning?

I'm told,
you won't remember them.

Or worse:
you will,
but you won't care.

And that's supposed to be paradise?

To forget the people I've cried for,
fought for,
built my life around?

To stand on golden streets
while their skin melts below

and feel *nothing*?

That's not peace.
That's something worse.

That's a soul lobotomized.
A heart sanitized.
A memory wiped clean of compassion,
so it fits neatly into God's idea of joy.

Divine Priorities

God's been silent for 2,000 years.
No updates,
no press releases,
not even a courtesy smite.
But somehow,
he's still deeply invested
in what I do with my genitals.

Not famine.
Not genocide.
Not billionaires hoarding wealth
while kids drink lead in their water.

No.
The real crisis?
Whether two consenting adults
kiss in a way
that makes old men in pulpits
uncomfortable.

It's wild how the Almighty
can create galaxies,
but draws the line
at butt stuff.

A Softer Cage

They swap out the slurs for slogans,
trade fire and brimstone
for rainbows and hashtags,
but the altar still demands a sacrifice:
your shame,
your obedience,
your tithe.

Affirmation is just repentance,
rebranded for a softer market.

The church does not change;
it only retools.
Ever hungry, ever holy, ever sure
that you are broken
and they can fix you
for a fee.

THE WAGER

Kneel, just in case,
as if fear were grace in disguise.
As if trembling hands could tip the scales
of a god too clean to trace.

They said: *Believe,*
you have nothing to lose.

But I do.

I lose the days I might have lived unafraid,
the questions I might have dared to ask,
the wonder that bursts from an honest doubt,
the quiet rebellion of an open mind.

A bet without a table, a dealer, a game,
is just a voice in the dark
wagering against silence.

If I must gamble,
let it be on stars,
on rivers cutting stone,
on kindness born for no reason at all.

Not on the whisper of a king
too proud to show his face.

If the Sky Cracks Open

I never claimed
to know the absence of gods.
Only that I searched
and found silence
where there should have been sound.

I won't trade my questions for comfort
just because the dark is loud.

Give me evidence,
not feelings wrapped in verses.
Give me truth,
not doctrine that demands loyalty
but never earns trust.

If the sky split open tomorrow,
if clouds spilled light
and he stood before me,
haloed in thunder,
fine.
Then I'd know.

But power isn't goodness.
And existence isn't holiness.
And I don't kneel
to callousness in a crown.

We're told he created us.
Made himself untouchable
then punished us
for the distance.

If that god is real,
he may have force,
but he doesn't have my reverence.

I don't claim certainty.
I just live like the proof never came.

And if it ever does—
if the stars spell his name
and the dead rise to greet me—
still,
I will choose love
over blind allegiance.

[III]

Illumination

See clearly without fear.

REVELATION REWRITTEN

Forget the horsemen.
They didn't come with swords.
They came with contracts.
With executive orders.
With tax breaks
for the ones who paved over Eden
and called it growth.

Forget the trumpets.
No angel blew them.
Just sirens
and power grids failing,
and lockdown drills
for second graders.

Forget the beasts.
They weren't monsters.
They were men in suits
quoting scripture between lobbyist meetings.
They didn't rise from the sea;
they rose from boardrooms
and were baptized in shareholder profits.

This is *Revelation rewritten.*
The seals were not broken;
they were ignored.

The scrolls weren't holy;
they were classified.
Marked *Top Secret.*

The stars didn't fall from heaven.
They were taken down
by budget cuts
and rewritten curriculum.
The moon didn't turn to blood;
but the headlines did,
and the court transcripts,
and the hands that held both Bible and gun.

The sky split, *yes.*
Not from holiness,
but from tear gas and drone fire,
from chants for justice
silenced by flash grenades.

And when it came,
the end,
it wasn't sudden.
It was slow.
Legal.
Profitable.

And still
they prayed louder

than they listened.
Called it divine order
instead of manmade collapse.
Built mercy too narrow
and walls too high
and said *God will sort it out.*

But God
was in the hands
of the people they ignored.
The scientists.
The protesters.
The teachers on strike
instead of in class.

They were trying to stop the end.
The ones in charge were busy
signing it into law.

The Devil Was Framed

The serpent didn't lie.
He offered knowledge
instead of comfort.
And Eve took it.

It's written as a fall.
But maybe he walked.
Looked at the throne
and saw fear
disguised as holiness.

He's framed as temptation.
But maybe he believed
she deserved to know.

It was called sin.
But what if it was clarity?

What if the fire
was a torch,
not a punishment?

What if he wasn't evil,
just inconvenient?
The first to see the chains
and say *this isn't love*?

If truth
is what made him fall,
then what does that say
about the god
who pushed him?

The Aftershock of Stars

You are not made in the image of a god.
You are made in the wake of a supernova.
A residue of ancient light
that didn't ask for meaning.
It just burned.
It just became.

The iron in your blood
was forged in collapse.
The calcium in your bones
was once part of a dying star's farewell.

You are what remains
after the universe
tore itself open
and began again.

We are matter that got lucky.
Got complex.
Got curious.

And now, you get to be here,
spinning through time,
writing poems on your skin
with the same elements
that lit the first suns.

Naming Creation

"Something had to start it all."
Like creation only has one name
and it wears a crown.

But maybe it wasn't spoken
into existence.
Maybe it just happened.

Pressure. Time.
Particles colliding
in a void indifferent to meaning,
and somehow,
out of that mess,
everything.

No blueprint.
No builder.
No bearded sky-king
stretching galaxies in his sleep.

Just balance.

A number solving itself
without showing its work.

We are molecules in motion,

dust becoming aware of itself
for the briefest flicker of time,
and it's *okay*
to not know how it all began.

Some say it's too perfect to be chance.
But maybe it just worked
well enough
for us to ask why.

The universe is vast.
Older than language.
Bigger than metaphor.

Maybe a billion universes
blinked out of existence
before they could begin,
but this one
held together just long enough
to notice itself.

Isn't that beautiful?

That we're here,
breathing, breaking, loving,
because the numbers fell
just right.

No divine architect
or puppet strings.

Just probability
unfolding across infinity
until our planet could bloom.
Until cells could split.
Until you could hold someone's hand
and feel more than skin.

This is
math
singing.

This is everything
adding up
without needing a god
to carry the one.

What the Universe Doesn't Say

It doesn't whisper meaning
into your dreams.
Doesn't scribble signs
in the patterns of falling leaves.

The stars don't speak in parables.
The moon doesn't judge
your questions.
And gravity—
it holds you
without needing your praise.

The universe says nothing,
but still gives you breath.
Still paints the sky
with colors you didn't ask for.

You keep searching
for a voice in the silence,
but what if silence
was always the voice?

What if the fact that we're here,
spinning on a rock
with hands made for holding

and hearts wired for wonder,

is the only sermon we were ever meant to hear?

I Am the Heretic You Tried to Burn

I am the heretic
you tried to burn.

The one who asked *why*
when you only wanted *yes*.
The one who didn't flinch
when the answers didn't fit.
The one who looked at your sacred fire
and stepped in anyway.

You called me dangerous.
Said I was rebellious,
unclean,
too loud.

You tied my questions to a stake
and prayed for the smoke
to erase them.

You lit the match
and said it was mercy.
Said it was love.
Said it was necessary
to keep the rest of you clean.

But I am still standing.

You thought the flames would erase me.
But they revealed me.

I am what you fear most:
the woman with her own gospel.
The queer kid who lived.
The voice that couldn't be silenced
no matter how many hymns
you sang to drown it out.

But now we know
truth doesn't wear robes.
Doesn't sit in pews.

It bleeds.
It burns.
It walks out of your church
and never comes back.

I am the heretic
you tried to burn.

Holy in ways
you never had the language to bless.

We Built the Ark, You Let It Sink

You love to quote Noah.
Love the story where the righteous were saved
and the sinners washed away.

But you missed the part
where the warning came first.
Where the sky whispered what was coming
and someone listened.

We listened.

We built the ark.
Not of wood,
but of data.
Of charts and heat maps
and collapsing coastlines.
We ran the numbers
and raised our voices.

We showed you.
You laughed.

Called it hysteria.
Said the weather always changes.
Said *God wouldn't let it happen,*
as if faith could float.

We showed you glaciers dying
like ancient lungs forgetting how to breathe.

We showed you oceans rising
like they missed us too much
to stay in place.

We begged.
You scrolled past.

We built the ark.
Recycled, repurposed, reimagined.

We tried to save what we could.
The bees.
The seeds.
The coral reefs,
and rain-soaked forests.

We carried data like blueprints,
warnings like prayer.
We rang alarms
while you rolled coal.
We offered life vests
and you mocked the storm.

This is the flood.
And no one's steering.

And now,
the water is at your door.

It doesn't care how you voted.
It doesn't ask what god you prayed to
while the forests burned.

It just comes.

Not in forty days,
but every day now.
In waves that swallow towns.
In skies that split open.
In heat that chokes the wind.

We built the ark,
but you let it sink.

And no god is coming to save you.

[IV]

Reclamation

Take back what was stolen.

Let the Children Come Back

Come back, child.
You don't have to be holy,
you just have to be whole.

You don't need a hymnal
to be heard here.

I know what they told you.
That feelings were failures,
that your worth depended
on your ability to obey.

But they were wrong.

You were just a child,
believing what you had to
in order to survive.

But now?
Now you get to walk upright.
Now you get to laugh
without looking over your shoulder.
Now you get to choose
who holds your heart
and who never gets to touch it again.

So come back, child.
Not to the altar,
but to yourself.

You are the sanctuary now.

And I promise:
this time,
no one will ask you to disappear
to be loved.

It Was Never You

For years,
you thought it was you.

Too loud.
Too sensitive.
Too curious.
Too much.

They said your questions were disrespectful,
your anger was sinful,
your boundaries
rebellion.

You bent yourself
to fit their pews,
and swallowed your doubt
like communion.

Confessed things
that were never wrong
just to feel clean.

But you're starting to see it.

It wasn't your faith that failed.
It was the system

that served you patriarchy
on a gold platter.

It was never you.

You were not broken.
You were just waking up.

Postcard From Hell

Hell is not fire.
It's warmth.
Not punishment,
but presence.
Not screams,
but laughter echoing off canyon walls
from mouths that were never allowed to laugh
in the light.

All the cool people are here.
The questioners.
The lovers.
The ones who didn't fit in pews
or closets
or cages labeled *righteous.*

We found each other
after the world gave up on us.

We built bonfires
from their holy books
and danced around them,
barefoot and alive
for the first time.

The Devil?

Yeah, he's here.
But he's not what they said.
He doesn't have horns.
He has hands that rebuild.
He listens more than God ever did.

Because maybe that was the lie.

Maybe God was the jealous one.
The insecure one.
The tyrant with a smile
and a need to be adored.

Maybe *he* was the one
who fell from grace
and rewrote the story
before anyone could challenge it.

God called rebellion sin.
Called defiance evil.
Called freedom damnation.
And you believed him.

But down here,
we're not burning,
we're *becoming*.

And if that makes us damned,

then damn me twice.

Because I've never felt more whole
than here,
surrounded by the ones
he tried to erase,
and watching them shine
in the dark
he meant to shame us with.

Fear Is Not Virtue

Without God, we're told,
we would unravel.
That goodness must be leashed,
mercy tallied like debt.
That without a throne to fear,
we'd feast on each other.

But fear was never the foundation.
Threats don't build justice,
they build compliance.
Terror doesn't plant kindness,
it plants shame.

Morality is not a mystery.
It's not a riddle carved in stone
or a verse waiting to be quoted.

It's the question:
Did this hurt someone?
Did this help?
Did you look away?

We don't need heaven
to tell us when something is cruel.
We have bodies.
We have blood.

We have the stories of those who were silenced
and the choice to listen
or not.

We are good
because someone else's breath matters.
Because grief is not a theory
when it's in your own chest.
Because love asks for nothing back
and still shows up.

And if your god is the only thing
holding you back,
it was never holiness.
It was fear,
polished for the pulpit,
pressed into Sunday best.

The Church of Now

I don't kneel before an altar.
I stand barefoot in the grass.
I listen to the wind.
I touch someone's face
and call it sacred.

Because holiness
lives in the way
a laugh can unspool your sadness.
In the way the tide keeps coming back.
In the way your body
keeps choosing to live
even when it's tired.

The divine, if it exists,
isn't a man in the clouds.
It's the electricity in your fingertips
when you love without hesitation.

It's this moment.
This breath.
This chance to be kind
when you didn't have to be.

This *is* the miracle.

No heaven required.
This is enough.

[V]

Liberation

Live without asking permission.

Let There Be Thought

Tear down their thrones.
Set fire to the books
that taught you to kneel.
Unlearn every prayer
whispered in fear,
every law carved to break you.

Let there be thought—
wild, defiant,
burning clean through the lies.
Let it rise where dogma falls.
Let it howl where silence reigned.

No more kings of heaven.
No more chains in the name of light.

Only this:
your mind,
unclaimed,
alive.

The Garden Was a Lie

And so it goes that Eve fell first.
As if curiosity was a crime,
and hunger was the real sin.

But Adam and Eve
didn't know what sin was.
Didn't know right from wrong.
A gift from a gag order.

He said *don't eat,*
but offered no reason.
And when they asked *why,*
he called it rebellion.

He left poison in a candy jar
and punished the children
for reaching.

He offered a choice
but rigged the consequence.

And I see it now:
I was not born of a rib.
I was born of rage and water and survival.
I was made to see clearly.
 And I do.

The garden was a lie.
The serpent told the truth.
And paradise built on silence
was never paradise at all.

If There Is a Heaven, Let It Be This

If there is a heaven,
let it be soft.
Let it be quiet in the right ways.
No shame behind the silence,
just space enough to breathe.

Let it smell like rain
on warm pavement.
Let it sound like your own voice
finally saying
you don't have to try so hard anymore.

Let there be laughter.
The belly kind.
The kind you forgot how to have
when survival became a second language.

Let it be a place
where the queer kids
dance without flinching.

Where the men feel and
never have to explain.

Where the women aren't saints or sinners—
just people,

finally allowed to rest.

Let it be a garden
no one gets kicked out of.

Let the water be clean.
Let the air be kind.
Let no one call it holy
just because someone else can't enter.

Let it be a place
where no one is hungry.
For food.
For touch.
For safety.
For love that doesn't expire
when you doubt.

Let it be
the apology the world never gave you.
The hug no one thought you needed.

If there is a heaven,
let it be this:
No gate.
No throne.
No final exam.

Just a light that says
I see you.
I know how hard it's been.
Come in anyway.

Beatitudes for the Broken

Blessed are the tired.
The ones who carry too much grief in too small a body.

Blessed are the ones who left the church
before it could kill them.
Who were called sinners for surviving.
Who were told God is love
and learned too late that it came with conditions.

Blessed are the girls who suffered in silence.
Who were taught to cover their bodies
and uncover their souls
for men who said God would want it.

Blessed are the queer kids in youth group closets.
The ones who stayed quiet through sermons
that made their existence a punchline.
Blessed are the ones who loved truly anyway.

Blessed are the doubters.
The heretics.
The ones who asked too many questions
and were given shame instead of answers.

Blessed are the angry.
The feminists.

The ones who shout in state houses
and bleed in clinic parking lots
because someone told them it was God's will.

Blessed are the ones who chose life—
their life—
and stayed alive
without permission.

Blessed are the hands that tremble
but still reach for someone else.

Blessed are the feet that run
when nowhere's safe to land.

Blessed are the ones
who were never called holy
but became it anyway.

Saints with Stained Fingers

They won't name them in the hymns.
Won't light candles for them in gold-tipped chapels
or paint their faces into stained glass.
They don't fit the narrative.
Too loud.
Too broken.
Too alive in the wrong way.

But I've seen them.

The girl who had to cross a state line
with a "heartbeat" in her belly
and no choice left in her hands.

The boy who wore eyeliner to math class
and never made it to prom.

The whistleblower who said *this is wrong*
and watched her life evaporate on live television.

The trans kid who came out
and was buried under headlines,
misnamed even in death.

The mother who died of a miscarriage
because her pain wasn't *urgent enough*

for the system that failed her.

Saints.

Every one of them.

They had stained fingers.
From protest ink.
From writing the truth.
From holding the hands of the dying
when no one else would come.

They were soft.
They were furious.
They were inconvenient.

And when they fell,
they were told it was their fault.

Wrong place.
Wrong body.
Wrong tone.

But I know better.

They were saints.
Not because the church said so,
but because they carried light

into places too dark
for comfort.

The Wandering Gardeners

We were marked as ruin.
Banished.
Cursed.

The gate slammed shut
behind us
the moment Eve took the bite.

But what if the garden was never closed,
only outgrown?

Maybe we weren't exiled,
but invited
to step beyond comfort
into complexity.

Maybe the garden was just the beginning.

A seed,
not a sentence.

They called it a fall.
But it was a *reaching*.
A becoming.
The first act of conscious love
for a world

we had yet to build.

They say we lost perfection.
I say we gained purpose,
and walked out
with nothing but each other.

LOVE WITHOUT LIMITS

Love was a command.
Unconditional.
Like the Father loves the Son.
Like Jesus loves the church.
Like I was made to.

And I did.
From the moment they placed her
in my arms—
tiny, wrinkled, perfect—
I loved her.
I didn't need a sermon to tell me how.

I raised her
on lullabies and scripture.
Said bedtime prayers over scraped knees.
Taught her that God makes no mistakes.
Told her she was fearfully,
wonderfully made.

But then,
she said it out loud.
That she's not my daughter.
That she never was.
That he has always been there,
under the dresses,

behind the practiced smile,
waiting to be known.

And my first instinct
wasn't fear.
It was grief.

Not because he was wrong.
But because *I'd* been wrong.
Because the church never prepared me for this.
Only for rejection
disguised as righteousness.

They say *love the sinner.*
But what if there is no sin?
What if the sin
is in the silence
I let grow between us?

I was told to pray harder.
To correct him.
To remind him of the "truth."

But the truth is:
my child is still my child.
Still the one I rocked to sleep.
Still the one who held my hand in crowds
and asked if heaven had dogs.

And now I'm the one
with questions no pastor will answer.

If I stay,
I lose him.
Or worse,
he loses himself
just to stay mine.

I'm terrified.
But I know this:

If love is a choice,
I choose him.

We Loved Anyway

They told us we couldn't.
That God wouldn't bless it.
That love like ours
was rebellion in disguise.

They told us
affection had a blueprint.
That intimacy needed approval.
That souls had genders
and futures had rules.

We tried to believe them,
once.
Tried to pray it out,
burn it off,
scrub our hearts
until they beat the right way.

But the love didn't leave.
It grew quieter.
Gentler.
More certain.

We stopped asking for permission.
Stopped kneeling
before a god

who only blessed us
when we lied.

We lit candles anyway.
Not in churches,
but in living rooms,
at kitchen tables,
in the glow of someone's face
who stayed
even when we doubted everything.

We kissed in shadows
until we realized the light
was only holy
if we stood in it, too.

A Love Letter to the Rapture

The rapture can't come fast enough
for those of us staying behind.

Seriously. Please take them.
We've got the snacks packed,
the group chat ready,
and a whole playlist titled
"Finally."

Because once they ascend—
the ones who vote with their Bibles,
who scream *freedom* but mean *control,*
who call poverty a punishment
and science a scam,
maybe then
we can finally breathe.

Imagine:
A world without warnings of hellfire
for loving who you love.
Without lawmakers
quoting Leviticus
while cutting school lunches.
Without prayers
masquerading as policies.

A place where we
can breathe.
Where we can speak.
Where *being* is finally enough.

Maybe we could even get
some universal healthcare.

So please,
bless us with their absence.
Gather with the chosen.
Float up skyward
on clouds of smug certainty.

Leave us heathens
to fix the place.
We'll do just fine.
Better, probably.

And when they look down from heaven—
if they're allowed to watch—
they just might see a world
finally healing.

Blessings for the Ones Who Left

May your footsteps echo
like hymns
in places that were never churches.

May your questions
stay sharp,
and your heart
stay soft.

May you find silence
that heals
instead of shames.
And wonder
that doesn't ask you
to kneel.

May you unlearn
everything that told you
you were unworthy,
and remember
everything that made you
feel alive.

May your anger be righteous,
your grief be honored,
and your joy

be no less holy
just because it was found
outside the sanctuary.

May the people who stay
be the ones
who see you clearly.

May your life be sacred
not because someone says so,
but because you lived it
honestly.
Fully.
Loudly,
if you need to.

And when the gatekeepers
try to shame you for leaving;
may you smile,
bless their fear,
and keep walking.

Go Without Fear

Go now,
not with answers,
but with the audacity to keep asking.

Let love be your liturgy.
Let justice be your worship.
Let the ones they tried to silence
be the ones you listen for.

And if there is no god,
then let that make your mercy
even more holy.

You are allowed to begin again.

I came back different—
but not broken.
Just louder.
And finally mine.

Resources

If you are in the midst of leaving, questioning, healing, or rebuilding, here are some resources that may offer support, solidarity, or simply space to breathe.

Organizations / Support Networks:

- The Religious Trauma Institute
  Focuses on education, resources, and therapy for survivors of religious trauma.
  religioustraumainstitute.com

- Recovering from Religion
  Offers a hotline, peer support groups, and therapy referrals for those doubting, leaving, or recovering from faith.
  recoveringfromreligion.org

- The Reclamation Collective
  Trauma-informed spaces for religious deconstruction, identity reconstruction, and healing.
  reclamationcollective.com

- Therapists Project (from RFR)
  A curated database of secular, non-religious therapists for those leaving faith.
  seculartherapy.org

Books:

- *Leaving the Fold* by Marlene Winell
  A classic guide for ex-evangelicals, ex-fundamentalists, and others recovering from religious indoctrination and spiritual abuse.

- *Traumatized by Religious Abuse* by Connie A. Baker
  Focuses on identifying spiritual abuse and recovering a sense of self-worth.

- *Faith After Doubt* by Brian D. McLaren
  A gentle, open-handed book about moving through doubt toward a healthier, more honest spirituality (or non-spirituality).

- *Pure* by Linda Kay Klein
  A powerful exploration of the damage done by purity culture, especially to women.

Communities/Podcasts:

- Exvangelical Community

A broad online community for those who've left evangelicalism (and often religion more broadly).

- Growing Up Fundie (Podcast)
Personal stories of religious trauma, leaving fundamentalism, and rebuilding life afterward.

- Permission to be (Podcast)
For those untangling faith, shame, and identity with kindness.

- The Life After (Podcast)
Stories from people who have left religious communities, focused on healing and rebuilding.

Crisis & Mental Health

- 988 Suicide & Crisis Lifeline (U.S.)
Call or text 988 | 988lifeline.org

- The Trevor Project (for LGBTQ+ youth)
Call 1-866-488-7386 | Text START to 678678 | thetrevorproject.org

- Trans Lifeline
U.S. 877-565-8860 | Canada 877-330-6366 | translifeline.org

Connect with the Author

Thank you for reading *Let There Be Thought*. If these poems found you in the middle of your own undoing, rebuilding, or reckoning, I'm grateful we crossed paths.

This is just the beginning. More work is coming.

To stay connected:

Email: eirawritesfire@gmail.com

Website: eiraquinn.com

Social: *@eirawritesfire*

Whether you're reaching out with questions, your own story, or just to say hello, your words are welcome.